Advanced Archer

How to Stay Calm at the Center

by
Thomas Whitney
Vishnu Karmakar

Center Vision, Inc.
Littleton, Colorado

ADVANCED ARCHER
How to Stay Calm at the Center

Published by:

5769 South Bemis St. - Suite A
Littleton, Colorado 80120-2008

Disclaimer:
No responsibility will be accepted for injury that may appear to have resulted from using this book. The user assumes all risks and responsibilities in using these exercises.

Library of Congress Catalog Card Number: 92-71391
ISBN: 1-881234-00-2

To Ciranjiva Roy
also known as Father

Acknowledgment

There is no way that we could mention everyone who has contributed in some way or other to the writing of this book. To do so would take more space than is available. The list would include a vast array of individuals whom we have encountered on our journey's. Each one of whom has added their own unique perspective or insight to our work. We imagine that they know who they are.

The following are some of the people that helped us directly. Ken Whitney provided art and archery inspiration. Candi Penn did the majority of our proofreading. Rich Barry did the art work for the front and back covers. Ted Whitney added editing help and publishing support. Donna Whitney was layout artist and desktop publisher.

We sincerely appreciate and thank all of those who have contributed to this book. Without their support and inspiration this book would have not been possible.

TABLE OF CONTENTS

Part II - AT THE RANGE

THE ADVANCED ARCHER

PART III - SPECIAL SECTION ON TARGET PANIC

PART IV - THE EXERCISES

INTRODUCTION

Who is This For and Why?

Although this book is written with the average archer in mind, this program will work for any one. Pros as well as beginners can benefit from practicing the exercises in this book. If beginning archers were to practice our program and learned to shoot with relaxed concentration, they would experience fewer troubles with shooting and they would NEVER be bothered by archery's most often encountered problem -- target panic.

Whether you shoot a lot or a little, this program will help you make the most effective use of your shooting time. When you utilize mental training, with each and every shot you will be learning more about getting 'into the flow'. When you can get into and stay 'in the flow' you will know the wonder and joy of effortless shooting.

Improving With Mental Training

When practiced properly there is no other method that will improve your shooting as much as mental training. Ask any archer what role the mind plays in shooting a bow and the usual answer is "archery is 90% mental." A mind that is tense, worried or nervous will inject THAT feeling into every draw, hold and release, but a mind that is relaxed and centered will naturally and easily allow you to shoot at your peak.

The concept of Mental training has existed for ages, students of the martial arts have used awareness exercises for centuries and so have those who practice the discipline of Yoga. We have taken the best of these and modified them to specifically fit the needs of the archer. These are simple yet effective techniques for increasing mental awareness.

What to Learn From This Book

With this program you will learn how to relax, but not just the normal relaxation, you will learn deep relaxation. From there you will go on to learn visualization and how important that is for helping to eliminate bad habits. At the same time as you practice the exercises you will begin to experience relaxed concentration and from there it is a short jump to shooting 'in the flow'.

If you were limited to learning just one thing from this book, that one thing should be relaxation. Without the ability to relax; getting into the flow, concentration, and visualization, all will remain out of your reach. Once you have learned the art of deep relaxation the rest will follow as a matter of course just as long as you continue striving and practicing.

➡➡ *A centered, relaxed mind is the MOST important tool in archery.*

Tips on the Flow

This program is about getting 'into the flow.' 'The flow' really cannot be accurately described because it is just a feeling. If you have ever experienced this sensation, and most archers have at one time or another, then you will know exactly what we are talking about. And if you have never experienced being in the flow while shooting, and many beginning archers have not, then think of some other area where you have experienced this feeling.

'In the flow' is a peculiar sensation or feeling or you could say *knowledge* that everthing is going along just as it should. You knock your arrow and intuitively know as you draw that the shot will be right on. The motion is effortless, the concentration is undisturbed and the result is as predicted.

When you are 'in the flow' you will KNOW when you are doing it right. You do not need machines or a computer or a videotape to tell you that you are shooting well. Those things can help you to see that you are doing something wrong but to fix it **follow your own feelings**. At the most basic level ''The Advanced Archer'' is getting in touch with your feelings.

PART I - AT HOME

THE ADVANCED ARCHER

THE OVERVIEW

The Two Parts of the Mind

In order to begin mental training a basic understanding of the workings of the mind is necessary. At present we will cover this subject briefly, keeping the explanations as simple as possible. One could easily devote an entire book to this topic, but for now a rudimentary knowledge will be sufficient. For those who are interested in a little deeper explanation, please refer to the addendum.

The mind can basically be divided into two parts - the conscious and the subconscious mind. The conscious mind governs the mental activities that deal with our immediate perceptions at any given moment. It is the center of our thinking process and makes the necessary decisions for all of our voluntary activities. One of its big jobs is the determination of right and wrong, good and bad.

One of the limitations of the conscious mind is that it can do or pay attention to one thing and only one thing at a time. To test this out try talking to someone and reading at the same time. Either the conversation will suffer or there will be definite lapses in the comprehension of what you are reading.

The subconscious mind (also referred to here as the intuitive or instinctive mind) controls the mental activities that are below the threshold of consciousness. It is in charge of monitoring body functions, controlling the correct muscles for any physical activity - walking, talking, and so on. It is in charge of the memory banks and dictates our initial responses to the many and varied situations we all face. It also acts as a filter for the conscious mind. Without that filtering process your conscious mind would become over-loaded and bogged down with the vast amount of sensory data that is being received at any one moment. As an

CONSCIOUS MIND	SUBCONSCIOUS MIND
Can do ONLY one thing at a time	Can do thousands of things at the same time
Decision maker for your activities	Supports those activities
Final say in what is right or wrong	Not concerned with good and bad, right or wrong
Tells the subconscious mind what to learn	Learns what the conscious mind wants it to learn
Acts on the information brought to its attention by the subconscious	Filters out unnecessary information and highlights the necessary or interesting

THE ADVANCED ARCHER

example, if you purchase a new car you will soon begin to notice other cars on the road that are the same make and model as the car you just purchased. The same cars were there before, but you only began to notice them when they had something in common with you.

Naturally this part of the mind must be able to do more than one thing at a time. In fact, it is aware of and controlling hundreds and even thousands of details at each and every moment.

Important Concepts to Understand

1) To Serve and Protect

The subconscious mind ALWAYS tries to serve and help the conscious mind. What the conscious mind wants is what the subconscious mind strives to achieve. If you want to develop consistency, then the intuitive mind will be doing everything it can to accomodate you. A problem arises, though, when an archer wants consistency one day and the next day the desire is for pinpoint accuracy and the next day a big buck is the object of the thoughts. In this situation the intuitive mind will not be given much of a chance to work on consistency before it is called upon to work on accuracy and then on that dream buck. The solution to this is to figure out what you want and then stick to it. (This will be covered in greater detail in Lesson 4 ''GOAL SETTING''.)

2) Blind Obedience

The subconscious mind does NOT differentiate between good and bad, right or wrong. To it, a good shot is 'good' only if the conscious mind says that it is. Say, for example, that you make a shot that goes exactly where you aimed even though the release was jerky. If you think "that was a good shot", then that shot becomes an example of the kind of shot for which the subconscious mind will strive. Even though it intuivitely KNOWS that the the release could have been better, it will defer to the conscious mind.

3) Learning By Example

The instinctive mind learns and then repeats what it has observed. So, when the conscious mind is tense, the subconscious mind learns that tension is part of the shooting process. The subconscious mind 'feels' when you are shooting smoothly and when you are not. It really does not 'know' good or bad, it just knows how the shot feels. The subconscious will always strive for the shot that 'feels' the best, but that feeling can be overridden by the judgements of the conscious mind. The trick is to be able to listen to what the instinctive mind is saying, and then free it to do what it does best.

4) Who Is In Control ?

From this discussion so far, you might think that while shooting your bow the conscious mind is actually IN control, but it never really controls the whole shot. The best it can do is control two, or at the most three, aspects of a normal shot. That is why it takes some time to learn how to shoot effectively because both parts of the mind must learn all the aspects of shooting a bow. Actually when the conscious mind controls EVEN ONE event during the shot, it will somehow mess up that shot - **every time**. If you do not understand this fully now, don't worry; it will be explained more as we go along.

The Central Idea

The instinctive mind can learn either good habits or bad habits from the conscious mind. Learning how to consistently demonstrate good habits to the intuitive mind is the real importance of mental training.

CENTERING

What or Where is Centered

In this program you will often run across the phrase 'centered mind'. Although the term is fairly self explanatory, it is such an important concept that it is worth further examination. First, a centered mind refers **only** to the conscious mind. The subconscious mind is always centered on what it is doing, which is usually several hundred different things at once, so one could say that it is never actually centered. But, **whichever** way you choose to look at it, the subconscious mind functions best when the conscious mind is centered.

The ability to concentrate and the ability to center your mind are closely related, yet there are differences. When you concentrate, you fix your mind upon something. Whether it is archery, an upcoming meeting, a movie, or simply a thought, there is always an object (or subject) on which to focus.

When you go about centering your mind, the focus is not on any one thing. If there is a focus, it is upon the feeling of relaxation. A centered mind is **completely** dependent upon a centered feeling. So when you read about the 'centered mind', think in terms of the thoughts AND feelings being centered.

> *The ability to concentrate is ALWAYS enhanced when the mind is first centered.*

Finding the Center

With practice anyone can learn how to center their mind. By practicing relaxation techniques and then tuning into that feeling, the mind will naturally center itself. The starting point and home base for the centered mind is the place where you are not fixed on any one thing, rather you are focusing on nothing except the feeling of being relaxed. From that position it is easy to move the attention from one thing to another. You will find your ability to concentrate remarkably improved when you start from this feeling. The idea is to center your mind, then move the attention to where you choose while still maintaining the center.

Holding the Center

Maintaining the center is the difficult part. For example, you get your mind centered and begin to concentrate on the target. Seemingly from nowhere, into your mind pops a minor disagreement that you had with your spouse, and you begin to feel the irritation that you felt then. The moment you feel the irritation, your center is lost; concentration is gone, and if you were on the range, the resulting shot would most likely be a bad one. To regain your center you will need to go back to the starting point. Unless someone is very, **very** experienced, they will not easily be able to move from uncentered to immediately being centered. Nearly everyone who strives to become centered must continually go through the process of relaxing, clearing the mind, and centering themselves at their home base and from there moving on to do what it is they choose. With experience, though, that process will become shorter and easier, until just thinking about the centering process will serve the desired purpose.

In the *Bhagavad Gita,* one of India's most famous books, a centered mind is said to be like the flame of a candle in a windless place. In Buddhist texts, it is compared to the surface of a calm lake with no ripples and no disturbances - perfectly tranquil and perfectly quiet. As you go about centering your mind you may use these images as a lodestar.

Centered Breathing

A calm mind is essential for:

1) Retraining the subconscious mind so that its' actions are free and natural.

2) Assuming the proper stance when it is time for the subconscious mind to act.

To begin mental training, it is **very** important to learn "Centered Breathing". It is the **best** place to start the centering process because among the physical functions over which we have control, breathing is the most basic. Just as what we eat and drink affects us, how we breathe also affects us.

Centered Breathing is a suprisingly effective way to center the mind; it is easy to learn, and the positive results are noticeable almost immediately. Plus, once you have learned it, you can use it to help regain your center anytime and anywhere.

In India, this practice is called *pranayama*; it is still practiced by thousands each day and has long been considered one of the more important practices for an aspiring yogi to learn. It follows that because it is so effective, it can also be overdone. In fact, in every text on this exercise there are warnings to the practitioner of the dangers of doing this exercise too much. (This warning is more appropriate for a country like India, where it is not uncommon for an aspirant to practice a discipline 12-18 hours per day. Using this exercise 3-4 hours a day, for a beginner, would probably constitute "too much".) For the typical American with his or her busy schedule this is rarely a problem, but the warning is required when talking about this particular exercise.

(For the actual exercise, refer to the section in the back "EXERCISES". It is the first one.)

THE ADVANCED ARCHER

THE FLOW

In the Flow

The ideal situation for archery occurs when the conscious mind is centered. The subconscious mind is then able to move freely and easily, unencumbered with tension and worries; and when the intuitive mind is familiar and comfortable with the task before it, a centered conscious mind will be calm, relaxed, and will not interfere with the working of the intuitive mind. When that happens you are 'in the flow'. The centered mind is quiet, yet ever alert and on guard to ward off any distractions that might interrupt 'the flow'.

Almost all archers have had moments of being 'in the flow'; shooting feels effortless and the arrow goes exactly where it was aimed. Professional archers are able to do this with consistency; partly because they practice more in a year than most of us will shoot in a lifetime, but the **primary** reason is because they have learned how to put AND keep themselves 'in the flow' for nearly every shot.

'In the flow' as it is used here is synonomous with another commonly used phrase 'in the groove'. While the groove connotes a fixed, routine pattern to the shot, the idea of flow adds the extra dimension of rhythm. As all experienced archers know, you shoot much better when you are into a smooth rhythm. Interfere with that rhythm and problems like target panic can result.

The Dam

The opposite of 'in the flow' is naturally 'out of the flow'. Everyone knows **too** well this feeling. If you have been an archer for a while, you will be familiar with what happens when you are running late and rush to get to the range on time. Your shooting that day will likely be much rougher than usual. AND the harder you try to get back in the groove the less successful you will be. This is a good case, maybe somewhat extreme, of being 'out of the flow'.

As an extreme example, imagine what might happen if while you were learning you **always** had that rushed feeling. With the conscious mind NOT centered and NOT relaxed, the subconscious mind would learn to shoot under tension; it would not like it much - remember it seeks a solid, stable feeling, and a body full of tension is anything but solid and stable. There is not much the subconscious can do, though, because a mind that is not centered will rarely surrender control. Thus, the shot the instinctive mind learns is tight, stressed, rushed and 'out of the flow'. The subconscious mind will never really feel comfortable shooting like that. When it does try to take over and run the shot, the uncentered mind will always be there interrupting the flow with a succession of worries and complaints, or worse yet, suggestions and well-meaning criticisms.

The Goal of This Program

The goal of this program is for you to become a better archer and thus enjoy this wonderful sport even more. It does not matter if you are a beginner or a pro, anyone can learn and apply the techniques in this book. To do this you will first need to develop a calm, centered mind. Then use that calm and centered mind to turn the intuitive mind loose and let it do what it does best. When you can do that you will know what it is to be 'in the flow' and with practice you will be able to shoot 'in the flow' more and more often.

THE ADVANCED ARCHER

LESSON 4

RELAXATION

Relax the Mind Not the Muscles

Whether you shoot with a compound, recurve, or long bow the idea is always the same - to put the knock on the string, pull back the bow and release. This moves the arrow at a precise altitude in a specific direction. It has been stated many times by Olympic archers, archery teachers and sports psychologists that "you shoot best when you are relaxed".

If you pause to consider it, on one level, that statement is a contradiction. A relaxed muscle will not be able to draw a bow or even pick up an arrow. Actually, to be specific, what those people are referring to when they speak of "being relaxed" is a relaxed **mind** while shooting your bow. And to be even more specific, relaxed here does NOT mean "come home after work, kick your shoes off and watch tv." What is meant by relaxed is being at peace, tranquil, without ANY tension in the mind. This is true relaxation, and the **only** way to achieve this state is by practicing it.

A Relaxed Mind Means Relaxed Muscles

Why is it so important to have a relaxed mind when you are shooting a bow? All normal muscular tension has its origins in the mind, and wherever you find a mind that is tense, you will **surely** find muscles that are tense. A tense muscle when flexed is not nearly as strong as the same muscle when flexed from a relaxed state. And a high-strung muscle cannot contract as smoothly or quickly, nor can it relax on cue (which is the key to a clean release). Each and every shot is composed of hundreds of different muscles contracting and relaxing, and the smoothness, or flow, of the shot is dependent on each muscle being able to contract and relax in a precisely orchestrated rhythm. Because relaxation is so important, you can easily feel the difference between shooting 'tense', or shooting 'relaxed'.

➡ *Relaxation is a state without tension.*

Relaxation as a Skill

The ability to relax is a skill, and like any other skill, it takes time and dedication to acquire. For someone who has never practiced deep relaxation, it is impossible to go into a quiet room, lie down and tell the mind to relax; it just won't happen. The mind will wander this way and that way, bringing up a thousand and one different thoughts: worries from the past, concerns for the future, problems in the present. AND the more you try to relax, the more tension you will feel as you battle for control. This will happen when you are in the most ideal environment; imagine the impossibility of doing this under the pressure of an important shot with friends and competitors watching. Even for a mind trained in relaxation techniques, it is difficult to achieve tranquility when under pressure. Whether you are shooting in a high pressure tournment or just about to shoot a round with a few friends, it can hardly be repeated too often that "the more relaxed you are, the **better** your shooting will be."

Trying Harder

Most everyone has probably noticed that the harder you try to group your arrows the bigger the group usually gets. The moment you try for that extra control the muscles will tense with the exertion of holding the bow EXTRA steady. With tight muscles it is much more difficult to get a clean release, and a greater percentage of your shots will go off the mark. Even if you manage to do well on several shots, tight muscles will never produce the consistent accuracy of smooth relaxed shooting. In fact, the nearly inevitable result of continued EXTRA effort is some form of target panic.

Trying and Doing

There is a major difference between trying to relax and relaxing. Trying involves effort, while relaxation is the cessation of effort. The harder you try to relax the farther away you will be. In the beginning, to completely relax might seem nearly an impossible feat, but with practice it IS possible. The key is to find a good starting point, and although tension in the body is a result of tension in the mind, the body is **the** place to start releasing tension. As your mind relaxes, your body will naturally relax, but in the beginning it is very difficult to simply relax the mind. The moment you try to relax the mind you will be moving in the opposite direction.

It is relatively easy to relax the body. This is crucial in the beginning. A mind unaccustomed to relaxing will find innumerable reasons NOT to relax. By using the rhythm of breathing and the movement of the muscles, the mind will be distracted and let the relaxed feeling slip in. Also, once your body is at ease, it will naturally communicate that to your mind which will pick up the feeling. When you get the hang of relaxing the body, it will give you important clues on the general movement towards relaxing the mind.

(The exercise for deep relaxation is number 2 in the Exercise section.)

GOAL SETTING

The One Thing to Learn

If you are serious about improving your shooting, or have a specific problem that you are trying to overcome (such as Target Panic), enhanced visualization is **essential** to learn.

Unless the mind is relaxed, it is difficult, if not impossible, to make your visualizations enhanced OR effective. That is why the relaxation exercise comes before the visualization exercise. Then you might ask, "Why is goal setting stuck in here, because once you become relaxed, then you can begin enhanced visualization - right?" You could, but before you actually begin visualizing, it is VERY important to know what you want to visualize; therefore, **you need a goal**.

➤ *Choose with care - what you wish for may come true.*

The Perfect Goal

The concept of setting a goal sounds quick and easy, and you might think that something so simple does not require much thought. Yet realistic goal setting is a valuable trait, one that requires careful thought and mental persistence.

The idea is to find a goal that is the PERFECT answer to your desire. A goal that is less than perfect, if achieved, creates at least as many problems as it solves; and if the goal is not achieved, then it may well have been a waste of your time.

Elimination of Target Panic as a Goal

If you bought this book because you have target panic, then the 'perfect goal' seems obvious - "I want to get rid of target panic - FOREVER." But pause for just a moment and consider these questions:

- ⊙ Just how long have I had target panic?
- ⊙ Is it going to be easy or hard to accomplish this?
- ⊙ How long is it going to take?
- ⊙ How is the best way to go about doing this?

The last question might be answered "I don't know, that's why I bought this book !!!" It is true, this book will help you to eliminate target panic and any other archery problems, but target panic manifests itself differently in nearly every person. Therefore the individual path to getting rid of target panic will be as varied as are the symptoms. This book can give you the general outline, but each person must chart his or her own course towards the ecstasy of shooting relaxed and 'target panic free'.

Keeping this thought in mind, and with the other questions still floating around somewhere, continue on with this lesson.

Precise and Realistic

The first step in creative goal setting is to determine just what it is that you want. Once you have a goal, the question to ask yourself is, "Is this something that is possible for me to achieve?"

There are generally two problems associated with this initial phase. One is not being specific. You might say, "Well, my goal is to improve my shooting". So, how will you know when you have achieved your goal? When will you be improved enough? A positive goal is very specific, the more precise the better. When you do reach that goal, you will KNOW that you were successful.

The second problem is setting a goal that is too high. If you set a goal that is very difficult to reach, and then fail, you will be taking a step toward accepting failure as a way of life.

It would be difficult to overemphasize the importance of precise, realistic goal setting. A goal that is achieved injects confidence and enthusiam into any activity, whereas a goal that is attempted and subsequently given up on, eats away at personal self respect. This can become a constant reminder to the conscious mind that it failed, making the next goal seem even more difficult and unattainable.

Attitude and Confidence

Nearly every child starts with the attitude, "I can do this", and with that attitude they exhibit remarkable success. But with successive failures the attitude usually goes from "I will give this my best shot" to "I probably will not succeed in this, but I'll try anyway" to "Why even try, I know I won't be able to do this."

This alludes to a subject that has yet to be discussed, but one that is critical in determining how well the intuitive mind functions - CONFIDENCE. This feeling will be discussed in greater detail in a later chapter, but you can easily see that setting a specific goal and then achieving it will give the mind a boost. "I thought about it, worked on it and did it, AND I can do it again!"

Keeping It Within   Reach

In this program several small steps are better than one huge step; this concept should be understood and followed closely, particularly in the beginning. The more difficult is the goal, the greater the reward and satisfaction, but difficult goals require experience and confidence to realize.

If you set a short range goal and reach it, there is no one stopping you from setting another short range goal and then another. In the world of the mind, several small successes are more beneficial than one huge success. When you are successful, and YOU WILL BE if you have understood this so far, you will be primed for larger and more long range goals.

Pre-Visualization

Goal setting and visualization are very closely linked. One of the best tools for determining if your chosen goal is what you want is visualization. Come up with a goal and visualize the successful outcome, then examine the resultant feelings. You will be able to determine many things about your potential goals just from visualizing their success. This is an easy way to begin. The real work of visualization, though, begins once you have decided on your goal, and you then use enhanced imagery to realize it.

Examine your potential goals from every angle. Be sure and take into consideration all those people who are close to you and will be affected by your plans. Before you finalize your goal, reflect on it over several sessions. Ask yourself, "Is this goal something that I will want in the future?"

> ➡➡ *The more clearly you know what you want, the better prepared you will be to accomplish it.*

You Are the Star

What you are actually doing here is creating a play in which you are the star actor. In this play, act by act you conquer all adverse forces to finally arrive at your ultimate goal.

It will help to write this down. Putting your goals into writing will help clarify them. It will serve to separate the impractical from the practical, while it plants the most important goals deeply into your subconscious mind, thus preparing you for the visualization exercise.

Dealing With Obstacles

Once you have determined your goal, it is time to examine what is needed to achieve it. Anticipate any obstacles; then plan your strategy for dealing with these potential hindrances. If, in the planning stage, your spouse is saying to you, "You are going to be practicing how much?" Look at possible ways to keep the peace and still have your dream. Consider any possible options that will balance the conflicting desires. If problems arise in your planning stages, this is the time to consider any possible solutions, even those that seem ridiculous.

ABOVE ALL, when thinking about this, maintain a positive approach. Nearly anyone who looks for potential obstacles will at one time or another become angry. This is a reaction to restrictive circumstances (even if they are only in your mind). When you feel like this, the heightened emotions indicate that this is a particularly important issue, and how you resolve it will play a significant role in the realization of your goals.

Anger

Anger is an intense feeling which has no legitimate place in the setting or the achievement of creative goals. This feeling, though, should not be simply pushed aside and then shut out. It MUST be dealt with, otherwise it will only submerge and come out stronger and more intense at a later date. To deal with an angry feeling, it first must be understood from whence it came. Anger and desire are closely linked, and if one looks carefully at the angry feeling, it is nearly always the result of a frustrated desire. When this is the case, the desire must be relinquished or at least temporarily put on hold; first get the feeling under control, then work on fulfilling the desire. There are many times when the only way to eliminate a recurring angry feeling is to express it to whom you see as the cause of that anger. But do NOT express it when you are actually angry, wait until you are calm and rational. Letting the anger out when you are calm will nearly always help to dissipate it.

Anger causes confusion. The only thing that succumbing to an angry feeling can do for you is to obscure the real problem and thus push any solution farther away. There is nothing that can be helped or changed by getting angry. When you feel angry, and everybody does now and then, first discover the cause and then endeavor with all your energy to diffuse that anger. In order to achieve your goals, any interfering anger MUST be dealt with and eliminated.

Keeping Goals in Perspective

As a final step in the goal setting process, visualize yourself having completely achieved your goal. Let yourself experience all the pleasures that come with that victory. Do not hold back; get into the joy of the moment. THEN - **let it all go.**

This does NOT mean that you imagine yourself failing; on the contrary, it means that you make sure your calm, peaceful state of mind is independent of achieving your goal. It may seem contradictory, but the moment you begin to make your happiness dependent on achieving a goal, you begin to set yourself up to fail. At the deepest levels of your being is the constant desire for what is truly best. A centered mind is so **important** that just about anything that gets in the way of that feeling (once it is recognized) will have to be removed. It takes a calm, centered mind to be able to shoot a great round of archery; yet the moment the great round becomes more important than the state of mind, the shooting will suffer until the proper perspective is restored.

➡ *The ability to see oneself clearly is one of life's great challenges.*

Should You F-F-F-F-Fail

Of course no one is going to be successful every time; failure is a part of success, and without it, success would not be nearly as fulfilling.

If you strive and work hard for a goal and ultimately realize that you will not be able to achieve it, you will naturally feel disappointed. Allowing yourself to stay depressed only imbeds the feeling of inadequacy deeper and deeper into the subconscious mind. The next time you work and strive for a prized goal, you will not only be dealing with all the normal obstacles, but you will have the added burden of a mind that feels weak and inept.

If you fail, it is natural to feel dejected; but immediately start analyzing what went wrong. Was the goal set too high? Did you have enough time? Did you work hard enough? This period of self analysis will give the mind something positive to work on, but it is imperative to look at yourself objectively and honestly. Examine not only what you did wrong, but also what you did right. A close friend, if approached sincerely, will almost always help you to see something you have missed.

Remember and reaffirm to yourself exactly what you did that was right, then pick what you feel was the primary reason for the shortcoming; concentrate upon that one thing, and use the feeling of disappointment to strengthen your resolve to, at least, do that ONE thing correctly next time.

A Note on Today's Life Style

One of our society's main problems is the memory of past failures returning to haunt us in the present. On television, in the movies, in advertisements, in the school systems, and in fact, nearly everywhere you look there are images of the perfect man, woman, and child. Those images portray exactly how WE should look, feel and act. Often these images are used to sell products and/or services, and like it or not, these images have become the defacto role models for all of us; yet there is not one single person who actually looks, feels and acts like these role models. The result is a society of people who are all touched to some degree by their failure to live up to the perfect image. Thus within everyone is a feeling that somehow, somewhere they have failed. Anyone who tries this program and sticks to it eventually will have to confront that feeling and hopefully overcome it. The best chance we all have for regaining our self respect is by seeing beyond those apparently perfect images AND realizing that within each one of us is a being that is alive and important, far more important than ALL of those 'beautiful' images PUT TOGETHER.

➤➤ *One of the keys to success is the ability to handle failure*

THE ADVANCED ARCHER

VISUALIZATION EXPLAINED

Enhanced Visualization

Visualization means to form a visual mental image. Enhanced visualization means to make that mental image seem as real as possible. Comparing visualization with enhanced visualization is like comparing black and white with color. During enhanced visualization you create your images and fill them with sounds, colors and aromas. This is much like being in a dream, except that in the dream you have no control of what happens within the dream. During enhanced visualization you can make the visual images seem almost like a dream and yet be fully aware of and in control of what happens. You will be able to visualize the feel of the bow, see the arc of the arrow, hear the sound of hitting the target, and appreciate the beauty of your natural surroundings. This does not happen overnight though; it takes practice, and it depends upon one's ability to achieve a state of deep relaxation. The more relaxed, the more you will be able to visualize. The more real the visualization, the greater will be the effect on your performance.

A Study in Visualization

In the early 1950's a study was done on the effectiveness of visualization. Researchers took 90 college students with no prior basketball experience and divided those students into three groups of 30 students. Then each group was told to shoot free throws and the results were recorded. For the next month, those in the first group went out and practiced shooting free throws everyday. The second group was instructed to visualize shooting free throws everyday, but to actually have nothing to do with a basketball. The third group was the control group and was directed to do nothing.

After a month, they were again tested. The first group, as expected, had improved; they averaged a 20% increase in shooting accuracy. The third group, also as expected, displayed little or no improvement, shooting 1% better. The big surprise was the second group; those who had practiced only in their mind improved almost as much as the first group. That second group improved their shooting accuracy by 19%.

What this study demonstrates is the amazing ability of the subconscious mind to learn to do something simply by thinking about it. In this example visualization was almost as productive as real practice, yet these students were not told to do anything but visualize. They were given no training in the best approach toward visualization, and none of them had ever played basketball before, so they probably did not have great personal aspirations to become good at shooting free throws. Imagine what might have happened if the students in the second group were inspired by a personal goal to improve, and then were taught an effective method of visualization.

Imagined Practice

For the remainder of this discussion, unless otherwise noted, when we speak about visualization, we will be referring to the special type of visualization called enhanced visualization.

In many situations, imagined practice can be as effective as real practice, and for certain problems it is actually more effective. It works because the mind and the body respond to a mental picture just as they respond to a real picture.

In today's highly competitive environment, visualization is almost an essential for any athletic activity that requires precise actions performed in a very short space of time. Examples of this are archery, tennis, golf, diving, high jumping, skiing, baseball, basketball and many others. Visualization aids in learning and refining repetitive motions; the more precise the motion, the more control and efficiency you gain. Visualization, UNLIKE actual practice, also enables you to work on certain areas of your sport, or certain problems that you might be having, without negatively affecting other areas.

A Typical Archery Shot

In archery, as in many sports, a great many things must take place in a very compacted space of time. As an example, let's examine the process of releasing an arrow. In a space of less than 0.1 of a second your body must perform many complicated actions. The bow hand and arm, while holding the weight of the bow, must hold the bow steady in three planes - up and down, left and right, and in and out. The head must also be held steady while the eyes focus on the point of aim. Meanwhile, the other hand which is holding the string and arrow must also be kept steady. Then at the exact moment, that hand has to be able to let the arrow fly without interfering with the forward path of the string. (If you shoot a mechanical release, then this last action is one of increasing tension on the trigger while holding steady - still a tricky manuever.) Immediately after the release the muscles of the body must absorb the resulting shock smoothly enough so that the arrow is not kicked off course at the last instant.

And this is ONLY the release. Think of the number of muscles involved. There are literally thousands of things that must happen to execute one shot. Naturally your conscious mind cannot pay attention to each muscle in the body and tell it exactly what to do. That is the job of the subconscious mind. Ok, that is easy to understand. But how about just one thing during the shot, such as keeping the bow arm steady for the follow through? Should that be the responsibility of the conscious mind?

How to Mess up Your Shooting

Have you ever noticed that when you decide to work on one aspect of your shooting, other aspects then suffer. For example, you resolve to pay attention to your release. The draw starts smoothly, then just as you start your release there is a hitch, as the conscious mind interrupts and tells the muscles in your releasing hand what to do. Then you must try to get immediately back into the flow. But this is difficult, because rather than retiring to its relaxed state, the natural instinct of the conscious mind is to seek confirmation whether it was done correctly or not. It is not an easy task to keep the conscious mind calm and relaxed. In fact, it constantly wants to be part of the action. If given an opening, the conscious mind will always make the most of any opportunity. (Like overfriendly next door neighbors-- once you let them in, it is difficult to get them out.)

If you are ALWAYS trying to improve your shooting by fixing this and correcting that, then the only archery shot that the subconscious mind knows is complicated, interrupted and distracted. The worst part of this is that the subconscious mind will never be given the chance to do its job in peace.

Practicing Wisely

Ideally, the best shot is one that flows in one continuous feeling from draw to follow through. The job of the conscious mind is to stay relaxed and out of the way, letting the subconscious mind do its job.

If devoting your attention to any single part of your archery game detracts from other aspects, the question then becomes - How do you go about improving?

If you practice, you will surely improve, and the more you practice, the more you will improve (up to a point). But there is practicing, and there is intelligent practicing. Practice will make you better; practicing wisely will make you better MUCH faster. To practice intelligently you need to do three things:

- ⊙ Understand how your mind works.
- ⊙ Be able to relax during practice.
- ⊙ Make visualization part of your practice routine.

How to Fix Your Shooting

Why is visualization so important? We have seen how concentrating on one aspect of an archery shot can interfere with the whole thing. With visualization, you can slow down your shooting and concentrate on that one aspect, and do it over and over until you know exactly how it feels to do that one thing perfectly. Then you can incorporate that feeling into your shooting, all without touching your bow.

If you attempt this in real practice, because of that increased attention to one aspect, you will nearly always notice one if not several other things that are in need of improvement. So, unless you have a very disciplined mind, your original idea of working on that one thing will become diluted with other things that need work. In addition to this, as you watch the arrow going off to the left and then off to the right for the fiftieth time that day, it becomes very taxing to maintain any sort of positive feeling concerning your shooting.

You will find that when you visualize something that happens rapidly, you will naturally slow it down, not a lot, just a little. But if you wish, you can also visualize it in true slow motion. Many times there are subtle problems where the cause is not obvious to you or even to people watching you. By observing the details in slow motion, usually the cause of the problem will reveal itself. Often a problem that was impossible to detect in real time, when observed in the mind, will jump out and become so clear that you wonder how you ever missed it in the first place.

The Beauty of Visualization

The beauty of visualization is that you can work on one thing over and over without getting distracted or discouraged. You can practice your shot hundreds of times, instead of 20, or 30, or 40 times. Visualization also allows you a unique view of each part in the whole process, and there are times when a subtle problem that was missed during practice becomes apparent as you slow things down.

Most importantly of all, when you work on the details in your mind, you free your self during actual practice to work on what is really important - staying *in the flow*.

Part II - AT THE RANGE

THE ADVANCED ARCHER

THE FLOW IN ACTION

Going for the Flow

This is a mental training program, and up to this point the focus has been on the mental approach towards archery. Now it is time to put all that you have learned into action.

Remember that the primary purpose of mental training is to get into the flow and remain there. From now on, whenever you draw a bow, the most important consideration should ALWAYS be to *'feel the flow'*. Getting into the flow (and staying there) will improve your shooting far more than any other single thing that you can do. So, whether your are in competition or on the practice range, strive to feel the flow in every shot and in every release.

Hangups and Fixes

The single biggest mistake you can make is to start tinkering with your shooting while you are practicing. (Unless you have HOURS in which to practice.) Anytime that you concentrate on one particular detail during your shooting you will be interfering with the flow. If you notice that you are doing something wrong or a friend points it out to you, make a mental note and then get right back to the flow. In the peace and quiet of your visualizations you can do the necessary fixing and adjusting. The next time you are out you will notice that what needed work will have miraculously improved without you actually touching your bow, and your pursuit of the flow can go on without interruption.

When you notice minor problems while practicing, it may be preferable to pause before a shot and mentally visualize the shot with the necessary correction. Do this a few times; then as you line up for the actual shot, center your mind and get back in the flow. It may not work the first time, but after a few tries the necessary flaw can be fixed. It is the best way to make minor corrections, far superior to attempting to make the correction during the shot.

This is the first lesson in Part 2 and it is an important lesson. It was kept short so that it can easily be re-read.

PERSPECTIVE

Beginner's Luck

Have you ever witnessed the phenomenon of 'Beginner's Luck'? An athletically gifted but rank novice to archery can pick up a bow, nock an arrow, and shoot a high percentage of good shots. This is something that can drive a hardworking, hard practicing archer NUTS. How can somebody just walk up and do that well?

Beginner's luck is based on perspective. A beginner to archery has no expectations or pressures. They have no idea what will happen; if he or she does poorly, it is only natural because they have little or no experience. Therefore, they are relaxed and shooting purely for the enjoyment of it. They do not analyze each shot, or attempt to figure what went wrong when they blow a shot. They are basically in the flow, and if it feels good to them they will often do remarkably well.

Contrast this to the hard working archer. They practice long and often, try hard to improve and do get better gradually. When this person shoots a round they have developed a LARGE set of expectations; "This is the third time I've shot this week, I'm due for a good round." Quite often they shoot under tremendous pressure. Some of the pressure comes from others; if you practice a lot, people expect you to get better. But the majority of the pressure is self induced and comes from their own expectations of how well they *should* do.

In addition to this, the hard working archer has read innumerable magazines, watched videotapes and has a mental list, at least three pages long, as to what constitutes the proper way of shooting and how to correct whatever is the current problem or problems. So, every time a mistake is made, they devote their attention to this detail or that adjustment, attempting to correct the problem. In the process they create more problems, and the end result is in an overall lackluster performance. Add to this a poor mental attitude, which often is the result of trying hard and not succeeding, and you have a person who will outwardly say they enjoy archery, yet seldom are they out there for the pure joy of it.

Approach

How you approach *each* round or *each* practice session is of paramount importance. Archery is a sport, and it is meant to be fun. Even if you occassionaly shoot poorly, archery can still be fun. Enjoyment can be found in simply being outside, or being with friends.

Archery is challenging. No matter how good you become you can always get better, and there is tremendous satisfaction in seeing yourself get better at such a demanding sport. You do not have to win a competition to appreciate how well you do. A good round, win or lose, can be satisfaction enough. But the REAL joy of archery comes from being in the flow, seeing yourself shoot with skill and confidence.

Maintaining Perspective

Before you even step onto the range, resolve to do your best to keep your sport in perspective. Endeavor to enjoy every valuable minute of your time on the range. If you make a bad shot, look around, take a deep breath, and remember to appreciate where you are. (You could be back at work.) You will then be able to completely forget the last shot and go on to the next shot. The same applies to a bad round. Everyone has good days and bad days. A bad day, if kept in perspective, will not seem so bad, but if dwelled upon, it can infect other potentially good days with the lingering thoughts of the last bad round.

Talking to Yourself

To help maintain a positive approach, pay close attention to what you say to yourself while you are shooting. When you blow a shot, do not start out telling yourself what an idiot you are. (Unless it is with a positive feeling. Some people can communicate with themselves that way, and it can still be positive because it is in good humor.) The important thing is to keep the humor level high and REFRAIN from getting upset with yourself.

Positive Thinking

In the 80's one of the big catch phrases was "the power of positive thinking". Many books, articles and videotapes were produced extolling the benefits of positive thinking. From then until now many people were caught up in the idea that all one had to do was start thinking positively and everything would shape up to be the way it was supposed to be.

Of course, for nearly everybody who tried it, things were not THAT simple. Positive thinking alone is not enough. Thoughts need to inspire actions, and the results of those actions must generally be positive. If no actions take place, there is very little change. If the results of the actions are negative, then it becomes increasingly difficult to maintain the positive thoughts.

Three Examples of Positive Thinking

1) Lots Of Positive Thinking

An archer hears about the 'power of positive thinking' and determines to give it a try. He gets all jazzed up and thinks how good his shooting is going to be, and each time he goes out he thinks all good and happy thoughts about his shooting. Because he is so up about his shooting, he probably will shoot better - at least in the beginning. But, if that's ALL he does, then the initial rush of excitement will fade; he will end up not shooting much better and most likely will be somewhat dejected. When positive thinking goes awry, the natural consequence is, "Why bother to think like that if it doesn't even work?"

2) Lots of Action

A second archer gets excited about this new way of improving his shooting and is **inspired** to action. He is so sure that he is going to improve, he runs out and buys a new bow, arrows, arrow rest, bow quiver and sight - the works. He starts shooting with this new setup, and his attention is diverted FROM his shooting to adjusting and tinkering with the bow to get the arrows to fly right. His shooting gets WORSE. He gets depressed because he spent all this energy AND money expecting to improve and now is shooting worse. He was inspired to action, but his actions instead of creating positive results actually had negative results.

3) Effective Actions

A third archer decides 'positive thinking' is the way to go. He realizes that the best way to think positively about his shooting is to become more centered. Along with his normal shooting he begins to do relaxation exercises. As he becomes more relaxed, his shooting gradually improves, and as it improves his overall attitude improves, and he becomes a TRUE positive thinker - one of those people whose thoughts lead to creative actions.

The Guaranteed Way to Have Fun and Improve

When approached with the proper perspective, archery can be used as a tool for fun and relaxation; after a round you can emerge centered and tranquil. If, on the other hand, you find yourself more tense than when you started, you should consider either changing sports or changing the way you approach it.

Remember that it takes patience and determination to improve at anything, and shooting a bow is certainly no exception. Be patient with yourself, especially when things are not going as well as planned. But do not talk yourself into believing that you cannot get any better. No matter how good or bad your shooting, as you practice and improve your mental abilities, improvement in your archery skills will naturally follow.

*Pursue your goals with patience
and you will achieve them.*

THE ADVANCED ARCHER

CONSISTENCY

Good Days and Bad Days

In the section on perspective it was mentioned that everyone has good days and bad days. There is a certain consistency in *that*, but what every athlete or sportsman strives for is the total elimination of the bad days, so there are only consistently good days. As long as we are human, there will certainly be days that are not as good as others. What we can strive to do is to make the bad days fewer and *not quite* as bad.

There are a great many things over which we have NO control, but we do have the ability to center our mind. The ONLY chance that we have for any consistency is to attempt to keep our mind steady. Attempt is the key word here, although we have the ability to control our minds, it takes at least a lifetime of work to actually perfect that control. Still, if you strive for consistency, it is better to struggle, sometimes unsuccessfully, with centering your own mind, than to be constantly blown by the whims and assaults of events beyond your control.

Slowing the Pace

If you recall, in the section on deep relaxation, the first step in relaxing the mind was to relax the body. When you are working on developing consistency, it is also useful to use the physical body as a starting point. One of the best methods for this is to slow your normal tempo down a little; it does not have to be much, even a pace that is imperceptibly slower will serve as a reminder of what you are doing. Make your new tempo slow and even. Long before you go to the range, pick a specific starting point, such as when you are getting your arrows. As you begin to select them, start to move slowly and deliberately. Then through the entire shooting session, try to maintain the same even, relaxed pace. As you move at this new tempo, you will notice that your mind will also begin to pick up the rhythm and move slower and easier. As your mind slows down, you will gain a new perspective. With a slowed mind it will become easier to relax, center yourself and concentrate on each shot. As a result, even if little else changes, you will notice yourself becoming more consistent.

Dealing with Bad Days

Of course, you will still have good days, bad days and average days. If you can survive a bad day, or a bad round, and still maintain your mental composure, it will serve as an example and a building block. The next time a similar feeling occurs, you will know how to deal with it. Using that knowledge, most times, you will be able to alleviate the intensity of that potentially bad round and minimize the damage to your psyche. On occassion you will not only mellow the feeling, but completely change it into a positive, productive round of archery. This is a subtle art, transforming negative thoughts and feelings into positive ones, but it is possible and the rewards are well worth the effort required. When you do this, you will be taking a major step toward consistency in your shooting.

Dealing with Good Days

A bad day requires special attention, but an especially good shot or good round requires as much if not MORE attention to the workings of your mind. Ironically, the most common time for a terrible round is immediately following an exceptionally good round. Flushed with the success of a brilliantly executed group, your mind will naturally want to be telling itself what a good job it did. It will think it now has the key and is ready for anything; but in the process of celebrating, it will forget all about pace, relaxation and being centered. Consequently the next round will be as bad as the last one was good.

Your ability to remain centered and tranquil will be tested by the bad shots, as well as by the good shots, and by the bad rounds and good rounds. Either of the two will be able to wreck havoc with a calm mind, but of the two, a good round is often harder to recover from than a bad round.

Why Do This?

If you strive for consistency, then you must take up some form of mental training. It is THE tool with which you can begin to exert control over your mind. It is only by practicing and using your mental abilities that you will be able to approach any kind of consistency. It is not an easy task, but just as archery has its successes and failures, good times and bad times, so also does mental training. In fact, archery is nearly the perfect sport for the application of mental training. The goal of a perfect round is almost as elusive as the goal of perfect control of the mind. But the real fulfillment and satisfaction comes from each new step forward, each step achieved as a result of striving and effort. It is in those small successes that the reason for attempting such impossible tasks can be found.

COMPETITION

Winners Are Few and Losers Are Numerous

Even the worst of archers is acquainted with the *thrill of victory*, that indescribable feeling of triumph and success. More often than not, though, the average archer after a competitive round knows the *agony of defeat*. You might imagine that an average archer would win about the same number of times as he loses, yet that is rarely the case. In competitive archery as in most sports, winners are few and losers are numerous.

You also might be thinking that in this section, AT LAST, you are finally going to learn how to be a winner, so you can go out and trounce a friend who has beaten you consistently for the last few years. But quite the opposite, this is not about how to win but how to creatively deal with competition. One of the easiest and most frequent ways to lose your cool **and** your center on the range is to get attached to, and even obsessed with, the idea of **winning**.

The Desire to Win

In many people of the world, but particularly in American men, there is implanted from birth the desire and the need to succeed by winning. The word "win" comes first from Latin *venus* "to love or charm" and then from Old German *winnan* which means "to struggle". For many centuries, man has loved to struggle against one another for some possession or prize, or matter of honor. We come from a long tradition of giving great importance to athletic competitions, especially to WINNING the competitions; to the extent of giving credence to the philosophy that 'Winning is Everything'. How totally absurd is this way of thinking. It is one of the more harmful ideas to have gained popular acceptance.

Today's professional athletes are some of the highest paid people in any profession. In the game of life these athletes can end up as dismal failures, yet they are famous and highly paid ONLY because they are winners in their particular sport.

Athletics & Sports

When the desire to win goes rampant, the primary reason for pursuing a sport gets lost. To back this up consider a couple more definitions. The word "athlete" comes from a Greek word of the same spelling which meant "to contend for a prize". "Sport" comes from the Middle English

THE ADVANCED ARCHER

sporten which meant "to divert". At one time there was a difference between an athlete and a sportsman. The athlete was a true competitor while the sportsman's activity was done as a diversion, for enjoyment.

Now that distinction is blurred beyond recognition. Sports IS competition. Part of the blame for this predicament can be directed at the physical education departments in our schools. They maintain that these programs develop physical skills, build team spirit, establish good sportsmanship, and several other excuses, but in actuality they exist to build winners. Of course, there are exceptions but for the most part when a child or young adult takes phys. ed. what they are taught is how to win, NOT how to enjoy a sport. The schools alone are not at fault. The basis for the problem lies with our society and its obsessive attitude toward winning.

Growing Up in A Competitive Society

Look at what it was like growing up in a competitive society; the natural athletes were and are the social heros. Even as early as grade school, during the spring rite of 'field day' the winners were glorified with rows of ribbons pinned to their shirts while the losers wished and dreamed that they were good runners, jumpers or something that could get them a ribbon and make them popular. The need to win is carried on to High School where the jocks still make up the elite of the social structure. It was and still is rare to see a homecoming king that is not a star athlete.

Effects of the Competitive Attitude

America's big three are baseball, basketball and football, all of them competitive team sports. Anyone who has ever played one of those, (or any team sport) and most boys who grew up in the 50's and 60's did, knows the devastating feeling of losing a game because they blew it at a critical moment. Even though the main rap was that team sports build character, there was not anything quite so destructive to a psyche as being the one that was at fault in a loss. Indeed, for many, the need to be a winner juxtaposed with the inevitable fact that you will sometimes lose completely stole the enjoyment from participating in ANY sports related activity.

Worse yet, that feeling of being burned out with competitive sports can affect one's attitude in adulthood. There comes a time when a mature adult begins to seek out sports, not with the enthusiasm of youth, or for the heady rush of competition, but more for the feeling of enjoyment that comes from exercise and the chance to practice being skillful in action. If the experience with competitive sports was frightful enough, then it is very difficult to regain the appreciation for sports as sports should be - a pleasant diversion.

The Winners

For the winners, on the other hand, they often take the winning attitude into college and further on into life and business and are usually looked upon as successful people. Most of these learned how to put winning into perspective and are truly well-rounded, productive folks. A few though became addicted to winning; whether in sports, business or life, it doesn't matter, their self worth is dependent on conquering other individuals. However, they are the real losers. They must have other people around to defeat, yet eventually they end up driving all friends and relationships away. For that type of person archery is not a sport but a continual battleground.

Competition and Its Proper Place

This is not to say that all competition is bad or that everyone should give up on winning and pursue every sport solely for the sake of enjoyment. Competition does have its place in our lives, and whenever there is competition, there are going to be winners and losers. Part of being a good athlete and well rounded person is to know how to handle gracefully both losing and winning, and that can only be learned from competing. Competition also provides a strong impetus for improvement. Few things inspire someone to work harder than losing by only a point or two.

With Whom Do You Compete?

An essential rule is to always compete with yourself, NEVER with anyone else. Aiming to beat someone else is an easy way to let the desire to win get out of perspective. If you have done your best, then you can at least respect your own effort, whether you won or lost. If you let the competition get personal, you will only be satisfied when you win. To win an archery tournament IS of some importance. But there are more important things in life, and losers on the archery range are more often than not winners in other areas.

Confusing Pleasure and Competition

Another problem dealing with competiton is less obvious and initially requires constant supervision of the mind to correct. This problem has two opposing aspects. One is the tendency to slip into a competitive frame of mind during a casual, relaxed day at the archery range. The reverse is to lose focus during a match in which you have chosen to compete. Whether you are in a tournament or you are playing to relax, you should always start and remain clear about the present reason for shooting. Are you shooting to win, or are you shooting to have fun? It is that simple; keeping them separate is essential but not so easily done. If your motives are mixed, your shooting will suffer. You will neither have the concentration and dedication necessary to win nor will you be able to simply relax and shoot a bow for the pure fun of it.

The Competitor

It is beyond the scope of this book to delve fully into the application of mental training for the pursuit of competitive archery. This book is written with the the average archer in mind. The following section is meant for that average archer who possesses an urge to compete.

When you choose to compete, to do it correctly requires intense concentration and effort. Although there may be some monetary reward or other prize for winning, the rewards for this kind of effort are mostly personal satisfaction, although occassionally there is fleeting glory.

Should you choose to compete, be prepared to pay a price for the potential rewards. If you are a competitor, it implies that you will have a chance to win. If you have no chance, you will be in a competition but as a non-competitor and this will not apply to you. All true competitors think they WILL win. The best of the athletes psyche themselves up to even a point where they KNOW they will win. At the present level of professional (and many amateur) competitions, even a fleeting thought of doubt can mean the difference between winning and losing. These athletes invest their time, energy and confidence into that single goal. Realistically, in any athletic competition there will be several who make that investment, yet only one will come out the winner. He or she alone will reap the rewards, while all the others pay the price of making that terrific commitment only to end up failing.

Losing is not ALL bad. It does build character and all that, but if you are there to win and do not, you will not be happy or content with a losing performance. It will naturally take a while to rebuild the confidence and energy to be able to go out and become a competitor once again.

For all but the serious archer, a relaxed, enjoyable game is definitely best for one's mental health. Yet there are certain occassions when it can be interesting and beneficial to test ones mettle in competition. If you choose to do this, just make sure that you do it consciously and whole-heartedly.

Do You Shoot For Pleasure?

For the majority of people archery should be under-taken because it is enjoyable to do so. It is far too easy to let the competitive attitude slip into a friendly round. When that happens the added pressure generally interferes with the flow of your shooting and makes it harder to simply have fun.

The next time you feel the desire to beat someone else come creeping in, try this. Go with that feeling for the first half of the round. Do everything you can to beat the socks off the opposing archer. Next, during the second half, change your feeling. Say to yourself (and genuinely mean it) "I don't care how well anyone else does, I'm only going to shoot for the pure joy of shooting." Observe your reactions to each situation. The majority of archers will shoot their best when the pressure is off and they are doing it for fun.

THE ADVANCED ARCHER

For the Winners and Losers

If you happen to be one of those rare individuals who shoots better when the pressure is ON, then you are a fortunate archer. You are one of those who wins as often, if not more often, than you lose - one of the few winners. With this fortune, there is naturally a price to pay. You must work very hard to keep winning on the archery range in its proper perspective. No matter how important archery is to you and how good you feel after winning, there are other things in life that are MORE important. Remember this, and you can survive being a winner with your self-respect intact.

For those of you who have to regularly deal with a winner, meaning that you are most often a loser, TAKE HEART. For peace of mind and general well being, it is actually better to be a loser at archery than a winner. Although it is hard to keep losing in its proper place, it is much more difficult to keep winning in its place. To be a perennial loser on the archery range, yet maintain your good humor and self-respect, requires a strength of character that is a result of being successful in other more important endeavors.

Whether you are a winner, a loser or a purely recreational archer, it does not matter. Mental training is not for learning how to win; it is designed for self-improvement. As you become a better archer you will become a happier and more well-rounded person for your efforts.

THE ADVANCED ARCHER

CONCENTRATION

The Basis for All Achievement

Of all the mental qualities or attributes that this type of training can help you acquire, the most important is the ability to concentrate.

Concentration is a skill that enables you to shut out all considerations that are not essential to the immediate job, whatever it may be. When you are concentrating on a certain task, you are not concerned over what happened yesterday, or what will happen tomorrow. All great athletes have developed this talent, as have successful composers, inventors, writers, artists or businessmen. In fact, all achievements (large or small) owe a great deal to the mind's ability to concentrate.

To be able to concentrate on the archery range is as much an art as it is a skill. When you are in the middle of a round of archery the ONLY important shot is the current shot. You cannot change a past shot, and any thought about an upcoming shot will only serve to distract from the shot at hand. You cannot think about what will happen IF you make the shot. You must think only of making the shot. Whether you are under the pressure of a friendly wager or in a large tournament, if you can maintain your concentration you will be able to play up to and beyond your normal skill level.

Concentration That Comes Naturally

Remember a time that you fell in love. When that happened you did not have to force your mind to think of the other person, in fact, you couldn't stop thinking of him or her. You were not actually trying to concentrate, but you were doing some of your best concentrating.

Relaxed concentration is similiar to this. Strangely enough, the way to control your mind is through your feelings. When you feel something strongly, that is what you will be thinking about. The more you think about that something the stronger your feelings become towards it. To function properly though, the mind MUST be relaxed. Otherwise, even strong feelings will only temporarily distract the mind from its preoccupation with concerns, worries, or its endless suggestions as to how to shoot better.

Relaxed Concentration

In respect to archery, when you 'feel the flow' concentration will come naturally. The more focused the concentration, the more you will tune into and feel each shot. To approach a shot and say to yourself "Concentrate on this shot" may work, but it is only partially effective because of the tendency of the mind to not ALWAYS do what is told. Before you shoot, use your key word (see Exercise 2, Phase 3) and remember the feeling of deep relaxation; then visualize the shot, and in the visualization see the arrow hitting the target (or visualize yourself shooting without target panic.) If you can do this, when you begin the actual shot your feeling and mind will be centered on that shot; you will 'feel the flow' and your concentration will be at its peak. The primary consideration here is to 'feel' what you are doing.

The Inner Feeling

Concentration is another one of those mental attributes that takes time, patience and persistence to develop. You cannot suddenly decide to concentrate and expect to have good results. Many archers already have developed a certain ability for concentration, but as they learn how to focus from within the flow state, they will come to know a whole new dimension in concentration.

There is no real step by step method to learning relaxed concentration, everyone must work out their own techniques. The keys to relaxed concentration are the ability to relax and the ability to feel the flow. The necessary drive to achieve this comes from inside. You must have a strong, genuine inner feeling to do what it is you are doing. You cannot fake or force a feeling for something or someone. That will not work any more than forcing the concentration. You can fool a lot of people, but you will not be able to fool yourself.

As you practice deep relaxation and visualization, your proficiency in concentration will naturally develop and expand. With experience you will be able to sustain your concentration longer, and the intensity of the concentration will increase until nothing short of a disaster will be able to distract you from your purpose.

If you have trouble concentrating, don't get caught up in worrying about it. If you must worry, then worry about 'feeling the flow'. When you can do that, concentration will come naturally.

> *If you do not feel good about what you are doing, you will definitely have trouble concentrating.*

CONFIDENCE

Half of Your Kingdom For This Feeling

When you practice this program there will come a time when you are on the archery range and you will suddenly be filled with a distinct, unmistakeable sense of confidence. You will know in advance that your shot is going to be a good one. There will be no questions or distractions, just a quiet self-possession. And to your surprise, the shot will be just as good as you foresaw. This is what it is like to be completely and totally 'in the flow'.

When you have that feeling, it is so real and solid, and everything seems so simple that you will wonder why you do not always have it. It may last for a few shots or maybe for an entire day, but it will leave as suddenly as it appeared, and you will be left wondering how to get it back. The feeling of being confident is so special that, if given your choice, you would never be without it. Alas, even for the very best players, confidence will come and go. What can be attained though is a little control over WHEN you feel confident.

What It Is and Where It Comes From

True confidence is the most difficult of all the attributes to acquire; and when things begin to fall apart, it is the first to leave. The feeling of confidence is a state of being, somewhat like sadness or happiness. Just as you cannot always be happy, you will not ALWAYS be confident. Anyone who functions in this world learns how to control their emotions to some extent, and with practice anyone can learn how to establish a certain amount of control over their present level of confidence.

Confidence and the Flow

The ability to get in the flow and a feeling of confidence are closely related. When you first begin to feel the flow you will not neccessarily feel confident, but as you practice and succeed in becoming familiar with the flow, confidence will not be far behind.

To get into the flow does not require that you feel confident, although it is much easier to feel the flow when there is a touch of positive self-assurance. But you will never be able to develop true confidence without knowing the feeling of being in the flow.

Confidence and the Positive Attitude

Before you can hope to achieve this you must have developed (or at least have a good start on developing) some of the mental attributes -- such as relaxation, perspective, consistency and the ability to concentrate. Yet, you may possess those mental abilities to the maximum, and there is still no guarantee that you will be confident UNLESS you have an overall positive mental foundation. Of all the things necessary to allow confidence to come in to your game, this is the most important. Confidence has its primary roots in a positive attitude and without that foundation, a reliable confidence will remain out of reach.

You are on the range and have a 40 yard shot downhill to hit a 3D target. There is a slight wind from right to left, and it is a tricky shot because the only possible path of the arrow is through a narrow opening in the trees. You tell yourself "I am confident that I will hit the perfect shot." Now, does that show a positive mental attitude? If you think that telling yourself that you will perform well is demonstrating a positive attitude, then you are partly right, but it is a VERY small part.

Of course with a positive attitude you have a certain faith that you will do well. But it is much deeper than that. You tell yourself that you are going to hit the perfect shot, and then you hear the arrow richocheting off one tree and then another as it disappears into the foliage. What do you say to yourself then?

Archery is a sport that can and will put anyone's frame of mind to a test (and a good test it is). If you can walk away feeling refreshed and tranquil after a round of archery where you shot poorly, then you possess a positive mental attitude. If you have trouble doing this-- and who doesn't-- it might be a good idea to go back and read the lesson on PERSPEC-TIVE.

How to Develop Confidence

Confidence is always developed gradually. In the beginning when a feeling of confidence strikes, it will seem to come from nowhere, but it is there only because of past efforts. A solid foundation for allowing confidence to grow is built by maintaining the positive outlook and taking continual small steps forward. (Rarely, if ever, does much confidence come from taking a giant step, even if that step was successful.)

Once you have felt the impact of a confident attitude, you will naturally want to do everything you can to further it. This you can do with determination and practice.

Practice and Confidence

Practice is one absolutely essential element in developing confidence. It is only with practice that you will develop the skills that will allow you to feel prepared and ready. (If you feel unprepared for a task, you will not be very confident in being able to accomplish it.) Practice here is not only physical practice but mental practice as well. Combining the two basic methods of practice will give you the best possible feel for your shooting. Whether you shoot for enjoyment or for competition, physical practice combined with mental practice will enable you to shoot while relaxed and centered. Only then can you begin to know the feeling of being "in the flow". When you release the arrow and are in the flow, you will learn to avoid the common occurence of clutching under pressure. As you do this your confidence in yourself and your shooting will grow.

Determination and Confidence

Determination is the other essential element, because it is only determination that will keep you going through the difficult times. As you practice and strive for a goal, there will come a time when success appears far off, so distant that it seems virtually an impossible dream. Nothing will be working as it was just a short while before. Actual practice will not go smoothly; you will hardly be able to feel the flow, and mental practice will be equally frustrating. During these times, only your past commitment to the goal will carry you through. If you allow yourself to give up here, confidence will remain a stranger to you.

When you run into these rough spots, every now and then give yourself a short, direct pep talk. Look at the positive side of the particular situation, there is always <u>at least</u> one, and become your own best advocate. Remember how important it is to maintain the positive outlook. Even if the pep talk is very short it will help keep your aspirations alive. A positive state of mind combined with your determination to succeed WILL carry you through, and when you come out the other side you can be sure that you will have taken a major step toward the achievment of your goals.

PART III - SPECIAL SECTION ON TARGET PANIC

TARGET PANIC AND OTHER PROBLEMS

In this chapter we will be addressing the specific problem of 'target panic', but these same techniques can be used on just about ANY shooting problems. The methodology is the same even though the problem is different.

With target panic, everyone must learn to recognize their particular manifestation of the problem and then discover their unique solutions. Hopefully, this book will give you understandable and workable guidelines for achieving this goal.

Forced Concentration

The primary cause of all target panic is improper concentration techniques. A broad statement, perhaps, but read on to see if it applies to you.

When the subject of concentration is brought up, the first image that usually comes to mind is of a face with closed eyes and a furrowed brow. The person with this face is obviously expending great effort and energy focusing on the task at hand. The perfect picture of concentration, right?

Well, it is the **accepted** way to concentrate. Take control and demand your mind to think about one thing. The problem is that you are asking the impossible from your mind. The mind cannot really be controlled by force. You can make your mind concentrate, **for a while**, but when you do this two things happen: one, you will never be able to experience complete and total concentration; and two, when you insist that your mind go one direction, there will naturally and inevitably be a reaction.

For Every Action There Is That Reaction

Every single archer, whether they shoot instinctively or with sights, has heard innumerable times, "Pick a spot and concentrate on it". So they pick a spot, and time after time they force their eyes to look on that spot, or they force the sight pin to stay on that spot. After doing that for several years the mind finally rebels and says "No More". When that happens it becomes impossible to do what was so natural and easy before.

In archery this reaction is called 'Target Panic'. You may have noticed that not a single archer ever gets target panic when they first begin to shoot. It ONLY happens to archers after they have been shooting for several years, although sometimes an archer who has shot intensely for a couple of years may develop it.

When Target Panic Strikes

What happens when an archer gets target panic depends on the archer. But there are basically two ways target panic reveals itself. One is an inability to hold the aim, and the other is the inability to hold the release. Of course within those two broad areas, there is a multitude of different symptoms that occur when the panic sets in.

Shooting With Sights

Target Panic most noticably strikes when an archer aims using sights. When shooting with sights, forcing the pin to stay on the target is an easy habit to acquire because, in the beginning, it is the quickest way to shoot well and get good scores. When you first start shooting with sights you do not have to worry about whether the mind is relaxed or not, all that you need to do is hold the pin on the target and let go. As you practice and gain experience you begin to understand that the more steady the mind is, the more steady the aim is. But, if you are in the habit of forcing the pin on the target, the harder you try to hold the mind steady the more it will resist. This is the beginning of target panic.

As you attempt, over and over, to hold the mind steady it will settle in to its own unique pattern of resistance. If an archer normally draws the bow with the aim centered and high, then slowly drops the bow until the desired aim is reached, a very common form of mental resistance occurs just before the pin reaches the target - the bow arm will lock. This is actually the mind saying ''I'm sick of holding THAT pin on THAT spot, so I refuse to let the pin even go near that spot.''

The other common way target panic comes out is: instead of refusing to let the pin near the target, the mind will refuse to hold the release once the correct aim is reached. The moment the pin hits the target, or even gets close, the mind will give the release command. This time it is saying ''I'm sick of holding THAT pin on THAT spot, so I will let the arrow go as soon as it gets close.''

THE ADVANCED ARCHER

Shooting Instinctively

Archers who shoot instinctively can also develop target panic although, apparently, it happens less frequently. Because they aim by 'feel', it is very difficult to detect an inability to hold the aim, therefore, when an instinctive shooter gets target panic the most common symptom is the inability to hold the release. Just because it is hard to detect does NOT mean that instinctive shooters are free from the aiming problems that sight equipped shooters have. Many times instinctive shooters will suddenly go into a slump and wonder what happened to their shooting, not realizing that they actually got a case of target panic.

Anytime you force your concentration there will be an equal and opposite reaction. Just as you can force the pin to stay on the target, you can also force your mind to concentrate on a spot. In the latter case, the reaction will come, but when it does it is just much harder to detect.

Treating the Symptoms

When confronted with target panic many archers will immediately start adjusting their shooting. They start shooting with clickers, having friends count, holding without shooting, and some even go so far as changing bow hands. These adjustments may or may not help, but if they do it will only be temporary. The mind will be distracted with any changes, but once the change becomes normal the target panic will return. More often than not these adjustments will only push the feeling of target panic deeper and deeper into the subconscious.

Other archers correctly attribute it to a problem in concentration and thus work harder at concentrating. If this works at all, it will only be a temporary fix because the harder you TRY to concentrate, the harder concentration becomes and the faster the mind will want to go in the opposite direction.

Treating the Cause

The only real and permanent solution to target panic is to learn the art of relaxed concentration. Naturally, to practice relaxed concentration, you first must be able to relax. Just being relaxed is not enough, you need to learn how to concentrate with your mind AND your feelings. This is covered in more detail in Lesson 11 in the particular section called "CONCENTRATION THAT COMES NATURALLY".

If aspiring archers were to learn relaxed concentration before they ever picked up a bow or even if they learned it as they learned to shoot, they would NEVER be faced with the problem of target panic.

Overcoming Target Panic

Once you get target panic learning relaxed concentration may or may not be enough to eliminate the panic. This depends on how long you have had it and how deeply it is imbedded into your subconscious. For some archers the habit becomes so deeply ingrained that even after they learn relaxed concentration, the feeling of target panic will possess them as soon as they draw the bow with the intention to shoot. When this happens it is impossible to maintain the relaxed concentration.

When you get target panic you get caught up in a self perpetuating cycle. As you feel the effects of target panic you get tense, and that tension makes it difficult to relax, which makes you try to push harder to make the shot. The mind rebels; you feel even more tense, and the feeling of target panic becomes more intense. After going through this cycle several hundred times it gets implanted so deeply into your subconscious that both you and your subconscious mind are convinced that you will have target panic for the next shot and the next shot and the next and the next...

There *Is* Hope

Although this is a very difficult cycle to break, all is not lost. By using visualization you can begin to get a feel for overcoming target panic. Of the exercises in this book, visualization is the most effective at helping to break bad habits. (The full explanation of visualization is in Lesson 6.) By combining visualization with the practice of relaxed concentration target panic can be overcome.

VISUALIZATION TO CONQUERE SPECIFIC PROBLEMS

Target Panic and Visualization

If you have target panic, visualization is where you can first begin to get a handle on overcoming it. When you get target panic you get immersed in a self perpetuating cycle. When you feel it coming on you get tense; that tension makes it harder to relax and increases the feeling of panic, which induces more tension. If you have target panic, all that you have to do to start that cycle is pick up your bow. And once you are into that cycle it becomes harder to break out with each revolution.

Practicing will rarely be able to break that cycle. The best you can normally do is to hold that feeling of panic at bay. By using visualization, you **can** learn how to break that cycle. ALL that you have to do is visualize yourself shooting without target panic. Sounds easy enough, but if you have had target panic for any length of time, we can just about guarantee that it will take some time and effort to do this. But it **can** be done by **anyone**, no matter how long they have had target panic. The key is in precise, realistic goal setting and then persistence in applying these goals during enhanced visualizations.

Target panic is a mental problem, and the place to solve it is in the mind. Once you have conquered it there, it is only a short jump (and a little practice away) from being able to conquer it with a bow in your hand. Visualize yourself without target panic and you are on the path toward panic free shooting.

Visualizing Your Panic

When you use mental imagery to conquer target panic, an interesting phenomenon will occur. You will find a tendency to have the exact same problem in your visualization as you do in real life. This can get pretty spooky because the idea is to imagine yourself **without** that panic. The mind's natural instinct will be to try to cure this problem by ignoring it.

You are cruising along in the mental picture and just about to release your arrow when target panic hits. So you replay it, and just as target panic is about to strike, you imagine the release and the arrow flying swiftly and surely towards its intended spot. You say to yourself proudly, "I did it; I imagined myself shooting without any panic." What you actually did is imagine yourself doing the impossible - skipping a moment in time; easy to do in the mind, but quite impossible in real life.

Conquering With Acceptance

The **best thing** you can do is to overcome your natural tendency to skip the bad part and actually experience the target panic in your visualization, just like you do in real life. Because you are in a visualization you can let your mind experience the target panic without the panic. Do not be afraid of experiencing the problem; rather seek to experience it fully. Because you are not actually shooting, the panic will not affect you as it normally does, and it will slowly disipate as you gain understanding of it. Eventually you will find yourself shooting without target panic in your visualization and then you are well on the way to eliminating target panic. You cannot FORCE yourself to be free of target panic; the use of force is generally what INDUCES target panic. Nor can you ignore the problem by skipping over it. You MUST accept a problem before you can go about working on it.

Pretty tough thing to do, but that is the beauty of visualizing it. Target panic is much, **much** easier to accept in a visualization. Because it is easier to accept, you will be able to see it and examine it. Once you can do this, you will learn how to discharge its negative effect AND eventually you will eliminate it completely.

➠➞ *The more you know about your enemy, the stronger you become.*

THE ADVANCED ARCHER

PART IV - THE EXERCISES

CENTERED BREATHING

To begin Centered Breathing, first make sure that you are comfortable. In the beginning a reclining position is best; as you become more proficient in this, you can do it anywhere.

Close your eyes and breathe deeply and rhythmically. Inhale filling your lungs from the bottom to the top. (Imagine a pitcher of water being filled.) When the lungs are full, exhale slowly from the top to the bottom. (Imagine the pitcher being poured out.) Establish a rhythm where the inhalation and the exhalation take approximately the same time, and yet you are not left breathless after several cycles. Then as you get comfortable with centered breathing, after the inhalation hold the breath for a count of two and then exhale.

A good rhythm to begin with is as follows: inhale on a four count, hold for two counts, then exhale on four counts. If you find yourself out of breath after several rounds, then establish a rhythm with which you feel comfortable.

Be sure that on the inhalation you are filling the lungs up from the bottom; this ensures that you are breathing with the solar plexus. Also, it is very important that you do not push yourself in this exercise.

As you get proficient at this, you can experiment with more advanced rhythms like 4-2-8, 4-4-8 or 4-8-8. These may sound easy, but they take practice, and the ones with the longer hold and exhale counts require that the practitioner be in very good physical condition.

This is a very simple exercise. Just because it is so easy, do not be fooled and take it lightly. This is one of the most effective and beneficial exercises that you can do. Because it is so simple it can be done anywhere, and the effects can be realized immediately. If you are shooting well, and something happens and you are in danger of losing your center, many times just a few rounds of centered breathing can bring you back from the edge and restore you to a state of calmness.

Once you have learned this exercise, use it often. A few deep breaths is one of the best stress relievers that you will find.

EXERCISE 2

DEEP RELAXATION

Preparation

This is a three phase process and each phase needs to be done immediately after the preceeding phase. It will not work very well to do phase one, take a 30 minute break, and then return and do stages two and three. In the beginning it should take about 45 minutes to an hour to go through the entire process.

Phase 1

First, start with centered breathing. After the inhale hold your breath for at least a count of one (a count of two is better here), and do this for a couple of minutes or so until you establish a rhythm with which you feel comfortable.

In to that rhythm you are going to incorporate an exercise that alternates tensing and relaxing your muscles.

Start with your feet. Inhale, and then while you are holding the breath, tense the feet and toes; hold that tension for as long as you hold the breath. Then on the exhale, release the tension; you can feel the tension leaving your body with the exhaled air. Next move up the leg and tense the calf muscles. Inhale; while the breath is held, tense the calves and then relax on the exhale. Next, do the upper legs and thighs. After that do the buttocks and then the stomach and lower back, then the chest and upper back. After that go to the hands and fingers and work up the arms to the shoulders and neck. Last is the face and head.

As you do this you will feel yourself becoming more and more relaxed. With each cycle feel your tension departing with the breath.

In the beginning it will be difficult to tell when you are completely relaxed. Therefore the first time that you do this, even if you feel completely relaxed after just one round, plan on about 45 minutes and go through 5 or 6 complete rounds. Doing this will establish a standard of relaxation for yourself, and from then on you will KNOW when your body is totally relaxed.

As you get more familiar with the method, it will become easier and easier to relax. With consistent practice you will notice that it takes a shorter and shorter time to relax, and in time you will be able to go directly to phase two, skipping this phase entirely.

Phase 2

Once you are relaxed physically, it is time to work on relaxing the mind. The way to do this is by remembering a PAST experience of calmness. So search through your past for a time when you felt a deep sense of peacefulness.

This is a special image and should be chosen with care; when you have the image it is very important to remember it vividly. To help do that, mentally answer the following questions; they will help take you back into that moment:

- Remember your immediate environment.
- Are you standing, sitting or lying down?
- What time of the year is it?
- Is it day or night?
- What kind of lighting conditions are you in?
- Are you alone or is someone else with you?
- What is going on around you?
- Listen and remember what you are hearing.
- Can you remember the aromas that are present?
- Think of the sensations that you are feeling.
- What does the air feel like?

During the questioning period, mentally answer the above questions, and then continue to ask yourself any other questions that would pertain to the chosen image. Work on this for a while and try to remember even the smallest details. One good way to bring that feeling to life is to pay particular attention to the senses of hearing, taste, touch and smell.

When you have done this successfully, that feeling of the past will pervade your present feeling and further relax you. As the memory of the past experience becomes clearer, the feeling of relaxation will become deeper.

Phase 3

This is the easy part; once you have reached this phase, all that you need to do is select a KEY word. This is a word (or two) that you will use to remind yourself of the present calm feeling. For example, if that calm moment took place during a sunset, when everything was bathed in a golden light, the KEY word could be 'golden'.

Repeat this word over and over to yourself while you are in the relaxed state, remembering the past experience. Make it so that the feeling of peace and the word you have chosen are so closely linked that one brings the other with it.

Remember the last time you were driving in your car and you heard a song on the radio that brought back such a strong memory that you could actually remember the smell,

THE ADVANCED ARCHER

taste and feeling of a prior moment. This is what you are aiming for with your KEY word.

This is the word to use when you are about to make a shot. It will move you into a relaxed state of mind. Use it when you are practicing and watch its effect on you. When you say the word it will bring the feeling flooding back to you. The more you practice this the better you will become.

The idea behind this is that from a centered mind will flow the perfect action. When there are nervous or anxious thoughts present they interfere with the natural ability of the subconscious mind. Whether it is logic, intuition or a combination of both that is needed, when the mind is calm the correct action will be automatic.

In time and with practice, you will be able to drop phase 1 and by just using your KEY word you will be able to feel a wave of peace and relaxation wash over you. As you get better you also will not need to repeat phase 2 as often, although it is good to practice phase 2 now and then, so as to keep your KEY word charged with relaxing energy.

Tips for Deep Relaxation

If you find your mind wandering, do not get into a battle with yourself; just keep patiently moving toward your goal.

When you are about to enter a high pressure situation, go through a brief version of this routine - take several deep breaths - use the KEY word - center your mind and thoughts - FEEL the flow and you will be ready.

VISUALIZATION

So you have set your goal and are ready to begin enhanced visualization. At this point get yourself into a position where you will be able to remain still for at least 10 minutes. In the beginning it is best if you are lying down; later, as you become more proficient at this, you can do it just about anywhere. (In fact, as you progress, you will most likely find yourself mentally practicing in the most unusual situations.)

First, make sure you are totally relaxed and that no tension has crept in. Close your eyes and begin centered breathing. Breathe like this for a couple of minutes, until you feel your mind is centered. If you have a key word, use it to help induce the feeling of deep relaxation.

At this point you should be able to slip into a state similar to a dream, where you will be able to tap the imaging powers of your subconscious. The primary concern here is to stick to the script that you created in the goal setting phase of the program. Immerse yourself in the mental image of your play and go through it step by step, act by act.

Be very careful at this point to avoid all negative or ambivalent images. Keep your focus on the script. In this dreamlike state it is easy for the mind to wander and lose focus; in fact, that will be the tendency in the beginning. That is why it is so important to have a PREPARED script.

What you are doing with this exercise is using the part of your mind where the conscious meets the subconscious. It is a very important and little understood part of the mind. In that place you can use the positive parts of each side to enlighten and train the unruly parts of the other side.

Because you are in a place where you can affect great change, it follows that it is possible for you to also make a change for the worse.

Some Things Not to Do

Wish for things

For example - "I wish I was a great archer" or "I want to be calm and centered". This is a dreamlike state and you are the creator in this world and not its victim.

Give yourself a pep talk

For example - "Stay calm and concentrate". You are the STAR in this play and if you cannot live and be your ideal - who else can ?

Battle negative thoughts

The best way to deal with negative thoughts is to keep focusing on positive thoughts. A fight only gives strength and credence to the negative forces.

THE ADVANCED ARCHER

Become discouraged

This exercise takes time and practice, go slowly but do not give up. It sounds easy, but it may take some time to acquire the skill to do this. The mind will play all sorts of tricks on you to avoid being controlled. Sometimes it is hard to get the two minds working together enough to even enter the dreaming state. When this is a problem, just concentrate on the deep relaxation. You cannot force yourself into controlled dream, all of a sudden you will find yourself there.

Some Things to Do

Strive for perfection and harmony

Start with simple images. Shooting on the practice range is a straight forward exercise and one of the best with which to begin. Do not expect to be able to run an entire play start to finish the first time. Practice at making one scene become real, then expand from there.

Incorporate all your senses

To begin with take a simple image of your play and enliven it with sounds, smells and textures as well as sight. The next time you are in the woods, use the KEY word, then spend a few minutes listening, feeling and smelling. Pay attention to the little details. When you begin a controlled dream, this scene will be a good one to use as a backdrop.

Rerun the script

Do this over, and over and over.

Strive for harmony and perfection

When There Are Problems

When you run into problems, you have basically two options; either work it out in the dream, or come out of the dream and review what happened. The former will work for minor problems, and there can be as many minor glitches as your mind can create.

It is not uncommon to miss a shot, or even to get target panic in the visualization (better here than in the actual event); sometimes all that is needed is a few minor changes, then just replay the scene and presto, everything works. Many times though, what caused the error will still be present, and when rerun, the same thing will happen. (See 'SOME THINGS NOT TO DO' - Become Discouraged). In this situation it is probably better to come out of the visualization and analyze what went wrong, or go back to the mental practice range, let loose a few shots there, and see if you can get back in the flow.

If, during actual practice you are shooting high, then the next time in your visualization the same error will likely be exaggerated. During practice you may not always see what is causing the problem, but when it is amplified in the controlled dream, it is usually easy to spot.

Also, it is not uncommon to experience that peculiar clutch feeling that often accompanies a pressure shot. If this is happening, it shows that you are doing well at making the event appear real, but not so good at following the script. Go over the script, and <u>with</u> supreme confidence emphasize to yourself the fact that you WILL be calm, stay 'in the flow', and then make the perfect shot.

Of course visualization will never replace physical practice, but the ideal practice schedule would be a combination of the two. To become adept at visualization, just like anything else, requires repetition and dedication; but the result will be a calm, centered mind, well prepared for your chosen activity.

➡️ *Imagining yourself doing something is a giant step toward actually doing it.*

The Two Different Views

Objective

In a visualization there are two perspectives which you can use, third person and first person. In third person you see yourself as a video camera would see you, from the outside; while in first person you are inside doing it, seeing it as you normally do in real life. Third person is most useful in getting an overall picture. If you are just starting and learning an activity, third person visualization can be very effective. Here it really doesn't matter who is the person that you visualize. If you know someone who has a classic stance, you can visualize that person. The idea here is to give your mind a mental picture of the ideal shot. With that picture clearly in mind, you will begin to shoot like that.

Subjective

First person visualization is the most effective when you are trying to improve on a skill which you have already learned. Using this perspective, you will work on refining all the myriad of details that go into each shot. If the last time that you practiced you noticed that you were not keeping your bow arm steady for the follow through, you can then visualize yourself during the shot with your arm in perfect position, over and over, until it becomes ingrained in the subconsious. Once the subconscious knows what the correct action feels like, all that you have to do is get into the flow and it won't be a problem any more.

THE ADVANCED ARCHER

Of the two, first person perspective is the most natural, and if you have done very much archery, it is the one that should be used on a day to day basis. Third person should be used occassionally just to keep the overall picture in mind, so as not to get lost in all the details.

OR
A VERY BRIEF TOUR
OF THE MIND

The Interaction of the Two Parts
of the Mind

Basically, your actions are dictated by the conscious mind; it leads and the intuitive mind follows. Learning how to drive a car can be used to show how the two different components of the mind interact.

For the beginning driver it is difficult (if not impossible) to shift, steer, accelerate, and brake all the while looking out for other cars or obstacles in the road. But with practice it becomes not only possible, but nearly every adult is able to do it easily. So, how does the transition happen?

The conscious mind cannot pay attention to both turning and braking at the same time, so what it does is focus on learning how to steer. As the conscious mind learns that, so is the subconscious mind learning it. When the intuitive mind has learned how to steer it will tell the conscious mind that it is comfortable with steering and thus free the conscious mind to concentrate on learning the details of how braking works. Once again, as the conscious mind learns so does the subconscious mind. Very soon the subconscious mind is doing ALL the driving and is even watching out for other cars, thus enabling our conscious mind to carry on a conversation with a passenger or think about an upcoming business deal.

Of course, the process is not *exactly* like this, the instinctive mind does not learn JUST how to steer, THEN how to brake, the whole learning process is accomplished in bits and pieces. It is fairly accurate, though, as to how the subconscious mind learns new things.

The Two Parts of the Mind and Sports

What this example illustrates is two basic modes of the subconscious mind; the learning mode and the flow mode. In the learning mode the subconscious mind learns and assimilates what the the conscious mind is concentrating upon. In the flow mode when the subconscious is comfortable with what it is supposed to do, it will play back VERY accurately what has been assimilated.

In sports the process is almost the same. The main difference is that in learning to drive, unless there is an impending accident, events happen much slower. In archery, to release an arrow, a great many things must take place in a very short amount of time. It is beyond the abilities of the conscious mind to oversee each event.

THE ADVANCED ARCHER

In the beginning, as the conscious mind learns the individual processes that make up each shot, so also is the subconscious mind learning. At some point in the learning process the subconscious mind will begin to feel at least partly comfortable with what it is doing. To have any hope of shooting well the conscious mind must then learn to turn control of the shot over to the subconscious mind. For a number of reasons, unless the conscious mind is trained to do this, it will NOT surrender the lead.

Also available from Center Vision:

Relaxed Shooting - Audio Cassette

On side 1 is the "Deep Relaxation" exercise put to music. Step by step it takes you through the exercise while you are listening to relaxing music.

On side 2 is the same music, this time combined with subliminal messages. This is good to listen to before shooting or before a big event. This tape is guaranteed to relax you.

Freedom from Target Panic - Videotape

A short ten minute videotape of archers shooting in the beautiful Colorado mountains. There are over six thousand subliminal messages displayed at the bottom of the screen and in the soundtrack. These messages are communicated directly to your subconscious mind and work to relax and focus your conscious mind.

Tincture of Arnica

All natural, herbal, muscle repair formula. Great for strains of muscles, joints, ligaments and tendons. When you use arnica immediately after an injury you provide the best possible environment for allowing your body to heal itself quickly and naturally. Works well for muscle soreness after shooting.

also - coming in January of 1994,
Advanced Running

The same principles as in the **Advanced Archer** but completely rewritten and customized for the runner. New ideas and concepts for using your mind to run better--plus a special section on injury prevention. If you are a runner, this is a book you definitely should read.

For information on any of these products, please ask your local archery dealer or contact

Center Vision, Inc.
5769 South Bemis Street
Littleton, Colorado 80120
(800) 735-0141